Jacqueline M. Pinckney-Edwards

UD1164BBA2081

# HYBRID ORGANIZATIONS:
## SOCIAL ENTERPRISE &
## SOCIAL ENTREPRENEURSHIP
### COURSE VI

A Research Paper Presented to
The Academic Department
Of the School of Business and Economics
In partial Fulfillment of the Requirements
For the Degree of Doctorate in Business Administration

ATLANTIC INTERNATIONAL UNIVERSITY
NORTH MIAMI, FLORIDA
http://www.aiu.edu

Jacqueline M. Edwards email: www.destinybound@verizon.net

ID: 1836307
Published by: Lulu.com

http://stores.lulu.com/endlssflw

ISBN 978-1-4357-0785-6

3

## TABLE OF CONTENTS

## INTRODUCTION

The emergence of the new class of *hybrid* organizations became visible in the early 1990's, even though its actual conception is found in the late 1980's. According to the free encyclopedia Wikipedia.org (2007), "[1]A **hybrid organization** is a body that operates in both the public sector and the private sector, simultaneously fulfilling public duties and developing commercial market activities. As a result the hybrid organization becomes a mixture of both a part of government and a commercial enterprise."

The examples listed by Wikipedia include "universities that provide consultancy services on a commercial basis, social housing providers that compete with commercial property developers, public schools that offer trainings for companies and hospitals that provide private medical check-ups" and more. Hybrid organizations as with other organizations have their highs as well as lows. Wikipedia states that "the combination of public duties and commercial activities can have significant synergy effects. But there is also the risk of unfair competition and that market activities could oust public activities."

Hybridorganisations.com defines hybrid organizations as "[2]an organization that operates between cultural orientations for example at the interface between the public and the private sector of society." Virtue Ventures defines social enterprise "[3]as any business venture created for a social purpose mitigating/reducing a social problem or a market failure – and to generate social value while operating with financial discipline, innovative

---

[1] Wikipedia, the free encyclopedia. Rainey, Hal G. (1996) and Koppell, Jonathan (2003) - contributors
[2] www.hybridorganisations.com
[3] www.Virtueventures.com

and determination of a private sector business." Both social enterprise and hybrid organizations seem to exist hand in hand in the nonprofit sector and fosters an environment of change that blends business, government and social concepts. Virtue Ventures go on to say that "[4]social enterprises use entrepreneurship, innovation and market approaches to create social value and change; they usually share the following characteristics:

1. **Social Purpose** – created to generate social impact and change by solving a social problem or market failure;

.2. **Enterprise Approach** – uses business vehicles, entrepreneurship, innovation, market approaches, strategic-orientation, discipline and determination of a for-profit business;

3. **Social Ownership** – with a focus on public good and stewardship, although not necessarily reflected in the legal structure."

According to Dees, (1998), social entrepreneurship consists of "[5]agents of change in the social sector, a mission to create and sustain social value, recognition and relentless pursuit of new opportunities, continuous innovation, adaptation, and learning, bold action not limited by current resources, and a heightened sense of accountability to constituents and outcomes."

---

[4] www.virtueventures.com
[5] Dees, J. G. (1998), reformed and revised: May 30, 2001 [paper]

## GENERAL DESCRIPTION AND ANALYSIS

Some have viewed nonprofit organizational hybridism as a paradoxical phenomenon. The pragmatic visionaries behind these organizations often face scrutiny and opposition because of their concepts, creative outlook, tenacity and commitment to their vision.

More than just collaborative, whatever the scope of this new breed in the third sector of society, it is certainly a marriage of the philanthropic and enterprising worlds that lead towards an empowered people with a definitive mission. There is a song that used to be sung in some churches, "I shall not, I shall not be moved. I shall not, I shall not be moved. Just like a tree that's planted by the water, I shall not be moved." The determination to succeed in their endeavors is intense.

So great is this hybrid organizational structural theme that organizations have mobilized across the nation, to investigate and report on their nature as well as the social entrepreneurs that conceived them. One such organization is the international nonprofit organization Aspen Institute located in Washington D.C.

[6]"**The Aspen Institute**, founded in 1950, is an international nonprofit organization dedicated to fostering enlightened leadership and open-minded dialogue. Through seminars, policy programs, conferences and leadership development initiatives, the Institute and its international partners seek to promote nonpartisan inquiry and an appreciation for timeless values. The Institute is headquartered in Washington, DC, and has campuses in Aspen, Colorado, and on the Wye River on Maryland's Eastern Shore".

---

[6] The Aspen Institute, Washington D.C.

Its international network includes partner Aspen Institutes in Berlin, Rome, Lyon, Tokyo, New Delhi, and Bucharest, and leadership programs in Africa, Central America and India.

Nationally, new organizations are emerging and demonstrating the capacity to be a major factor in the development of social and economic change. "[7]Many of these institutions, such as nonprofits generating significant fee-based revenue, community development corporations, and employee-owned firms, are hybrid organizations that blend governmental, nonprofit, and business values and strategies" according to The Aspen Institute.

"To better understand these emerging hybrids, the Nonprofit Sector Research Fund of the Aspen Institute has funded the Democracy Collaborative at the University of Maryland to undertake a new research project, New and Emerging Organizational Forms for Advancing Social Purposes. The study will map the broad range of emerging organizations in the United States and highlight how they address social problems by cultivating new sources of funding and promoting community-based activities that anchor jobs and foster local democratic practices."

Another organization examining social change is The Journal of Social Change sponsored by Walden University. Jim Goes, editor of the journal stated, "[8]By any measure, at the turn of the new millennium we find ourselves awash in change". There is great power in new ideas. David Bornstein (2004) writes, "[9]What business entrepreneurs

---

[7] The Aspen Institute, Washington, D.C.
[8] Goes, Jim (July 2006) editor – The Journal of Social Change , Walden University
[9] Bornstein, David (2004).

are to the economy, entrepreneurs are to social change. They are the driven, creative individuals who question the status quo, exploit new opportunities, refuse to give up – and remake the world for the better". Social entrepreneurs are providing and fostering an atmosphere for the search of excellence in the nonprofit division of the world. Truly, the concepts of hybridism, social enterprise and social entrepreneurship are taking the world by storm because of the almost overwhelming response to globalized social deficits.

Seemingly, it has been common place to study the methods, habits, orientations, and propensities of business entrepreneurs. But the study of social entrepreneurs has been virtually ignored until recently. According to Bornstein, (2004), this has not been for the lack of appropriate examples. He states, "[10]in the United States, an abbreviated list of well-known innovators might include: William Lloyd Garrison (abolition), Gifford Pinchot (environmental conservation and management), Horace Mann (public education reform), Susan B. Anthony (women's voting rights), Jane Addams (social welfare and juvenile justice), Asa Philip Randolph (labor rights for African Americans), and Ralph Nader (consumer protection). Much has been written about the various movements these people helped to build, their methods have not received the rigorous, cross-industry scrutiny that is common to the study of business entrepreneurs". Mr. Bornstein believes that "the difference in treatment between the two entrepreneurs reflect different attitudes about the role of individuals in the business and social arenas". He states, "In the business sector, individuals have long been recognized as engines of change. It was only a few decades after Adam Smith published *The Wealth of Nations* in 1776, which set down the basic tenets of market-based economics, that Jean-Baptiste Say identified the

---

[10] Bornstein, David (2004)

special role of entrepreneurs". Contrastingly, theoretical concepts of social change have focused primarily on "how ideas move people than on how people move ideas[11]".

As the times are changing tremendously in today's economics, there are people who are and will stand in the forefront of innovation where social change is concerned. It appears that the 'movers and shakers' of the social welfare revolution, will be the very people that are surrounded by it. For example, [12]Vera Cordeiro is a physician who lives in Brazil and is compared somewhat to Florence Nightingale. Tens of millions of Brazilians live in urban slums and suffer all sorts of deprivation including housing, clean water, and proper sanitation. Millions of children are stunted from chronic malnutrition.[13] Dr. Cordeiro founded Renascer in 1991, while she was working in the pediatric ward of Hospital da Lagoa, a public hospital in Rio, because she could not bear to see so many children discharged only to return weeks later, sick again according to Bornstein (2004). It made no sense to discharge a poor child back to the slums without follow-up care. That is the norm but Dr. Cordeiro seeks to change that. "To her, health and social conditions are two sides of the same coin". As of the publishing of Bornstein's book, Dr. Cordeiro has extended her work to fourteen public hospitals in Rio de Janeiro, Sao Paulo, and Recife, bringing direct benefits to 20,000 children and influencing a growing circle of medical practitioners. Her goal is to carry Renascer to every public hospital in Brazil. "Necessity is the mother of invention".[14]

---

[11] Bornstein, David (2004)
[12] Bornstein, David (2004)
[13] UNICEF, *State of the World's Children 2000* (New York: United Nations Publications), 23-35. More than 40 million Brazilians do not have access to safe water; more than 50 million are without access to adequate sanitation; 11 percent of children are stunted.
[14] A need or problem encourages creative efforts to meet the need or solve the problem. This saying appears in the dialogue *Republic,* by the ancient Greek philosopher Plato.

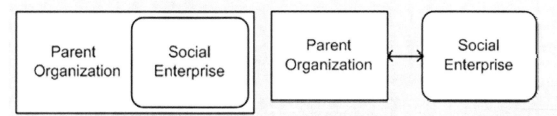

# Organizational Structure

A social enterprise may be structured as a department, program or profit center within a nonprofit and lack legal definition from its parent organization. It may also be a subsidiary of its nonprofit parent, registered either as a for-profit or nonprofit. Many organizations use a mix of different structures simultaneously.

The following diagrams illustrate the social enterprise structure vis-à-vis its relationship to the parent organization.

## Structured Internally

Social enterprise is structured as a department or profit center within the parent organization. The social enterprise may (or may not) physically share space with the parent. From a legal, financial, management, and governance perspective the enterprise is internal to its nonprofit parent. Systems, back office, staff, and leadership are integrated.

Any of the operational models can be structured internally within the parent organization; however, embedded and integrated social enterprises are the most common forms using this structure.

## Structured as a Separate Entity

Social enterprise is structured as a separate legal entity, either a for-profit or a nonprofit. In this case, the social enterprise may or may not physically share space with the parent. From a legal, financial, management, and governance perspective the enterprise is external to its nonprofit parent. If staff, overhead, or back office is shared, this is done so on a formal (contractual) basis as a business relationship. .

Any of the operational models can be structured as a separate entity from the parent organization; however, integrated and external social enterprises are the most common forms using this structure.

## Structured as the Same Entity

**Social Enterprise** Social enterprise is the same entity as the parent organization, meaning functionally that there is NO parent or host organization, rather the social enterprise is the only activity of the organization. There is no delineation between program, administrative and infrastructure aspects indicating the existence of two or more types of activities. This type of social enterprise may evolve into one of the other structures by adding new enterprises or social programs.

<u>Embedded</u> social enterprises are the most common form using this structure.

Legal Structure
**Read more about:** Social Enterprise Structures

Powering social change with entrepreneurship

**Virtue Ventures** is a small, innovative firm committed to furthering the field of social entrepreneurship through <u>action-research</u>, <u>technical services</u> and our own <u>initiatives</u>.

Our practitioner-focused and mission-centered <u>approach</u> stems from being a creative team rooted in industry: Virtue Ventures' <u>team</u> has first-hand experience designing, launching and managing social enterprises and nonprofit agencies. We have worked with literally hundreds of nonprofits and social enterprises, spanning sectors and industries in <u>35 countries worldwide</u>.

Since its incorporation in 2000, Virtue Ventures has received accolades for its high-quality services and excellent products. We bring unique functional experience and textured understanding of the nonprofit operating environment that is critical to rendering sound professional services customized to the needs of our clients.

THE ASPEN INSTITUTE
Timeless values, enlightened leadership

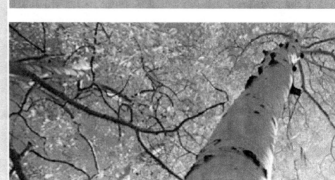

Nonprofit Sector Research Fund Supports Study of Hybrid Organizations Seeking Social and Economic Change

**Washington, DC, April 27, 2004** Across the country, new institutions with the potential to contribute to social and economic change have begun to multiply in recent years. Many of these institutions, such as nonprofits generating significant fee-based revenue, community development corporations, and employee-owned firms, are hybrid organizations that blend governmental, nonprofit, and business values and strategies.

To better understand these emerging hybrids, the Nonprofit Sector Research Fund of the Aspen Institute has funded the Democracy Collaborative at the University of Maryland to undertake a new research project, New and Emerging Organizational Forms for Advancing Social Purposes. The study will map the broad range of emerging organizations in the United States and highlight how they address social problems by cultivating new sources of funding and promoting community-based activities that anchor jobs and foster local democratic practices.

These emerging institutional forms are the result, at least in part, of the ongoing fiscal squeeze and steadily growing pressure on the traditional, governmental tax and spend solutions to community problems, said Alan J. Abramson, Director of the Nonprofit Sector Research Fund. This study will map the new organizational landscape and identify important public policy, management, and other issues associated with the expansion of the hybrid forms, he added.

Designed to be relevant for practitioners, policymakers, and the media, the Democracy Collaborative report will offer descriptive statistics on hybrid institutions, discuss how current and proposed tax policies may affect these emerging organizations, and identify similar international developments.

This important work will allow people from different fields to better serve communities worldwide. New organizational forms that change the nature of asset and wealth ownership are likely to dominate the next stage of development, said Gar Alperovitz, Lionel R. Bauman Professor of Political Economy at the University of Maryland. Such efforts also anchor jobs and contribute in many ways to the financing of critical services.

Organizational forms to be studied include traditional nonprofits that use business activities to generate resources, employee-owned businesses, community development corporations, community land trusts, and municipally-owned businesses. (One example: a small California town operates a cable TV system that charges users 36 percent less than competitors and channels five percent of gross earnings to city revenues.) The efforts of these institutions

share certain key principles. In different ways, they change the nature of as
and wealth ownership to help serve social goals and offer new ways to fina
services. More broadly, many of the models also help achieve greater lc
democratic accountability.

The Nonprofit Sector Research Fund (www.nonprofitresearch.org) v
established in 1991 to increase understanding of the nonprofit sector a
philanthropy. To do so, it works with a broad range of partners to iden
priority research topics, support research and dialogue on these topics, a
communicate research findings to appropriate audiences. Since 1991,
Nonprofit Sector Research Fund has awarded a total of $10 million to supp
400 research projects on a broad range of nonprofit topics.

The Aspen Institute is an international non-profit organization founded in 19
Its mission is to foster enlightened leadership, the appreciation of timeless id
and values, and open-minded dialogue on contemporary issues. Thro
seminars, policy programs, conferences and leadership development initiativ
the Institute and its international partners seek to promote the pursuit
common ground and deeper understanding in a nonpartisan and non-ideolog
setting. The Institute is headquartered in Washington, DC, and has campuse
Aspen, Colorado, and on the Wye River on Maryland's Eastern Shore.
international network includes partner Aspen Institutes in Berlin, Rome, Ly
Tokyo and New Delhi, and leadership programs in Africa

.
###

## About the Aspen Institute

**The Aspen Institute**, founded in 1950, is an international nonprofit organization dedicated to fostering
enlightened leadership and open-minded dialogue. Through seminars, policy programs, conferences and
leadership development initiatives, the Institute and its international partners seek to promote
nonpartisan inquiry and an appreciation for timeless values. The Institute is headquartered in Washington,
DC, and has campuses in Aspen, Colorado, and on the Wye River on Maryland's Eastern Shore. Its
international network includes partner Aspen Institutes in Berlin, Rome, Lyon, Tokyo, New Delhi, and
Bucharest, and leadership programs in Africa, Central America and India.

## Letter from Walter Isaacson

 Dear Aspen Friends and Partners,

At certain points in our lives, many of us feel the need to reflect on what it takes to lead a life that is good, useful, worthy, and meaningful. Perhaps we have noticed ourselves trimming our principles and making too many compromises in our careers, and we want to reconnect with our values. Or perhaps we yearn, in a world filled with clashing opinions, to understand the great ideas and ideals that have competed throughout the progress of civilization.

Aspen's seminars, programs and leadership initiatives offer a chance for restorative reflection on the meaning of the good life, leadership, and sound public policy based on nonpartisan principles and timeless ideas. The endeavor is particularly relevant today. We have passed through a period in the 1990s when we saw the consequences, in both the business and political arenas, of becoming unhinged from underlying values. We face a world in which the biggest threat, to nations and to communities, is a lack of tolerance and understanding.

Our core mission is to foster enlightened leadership and open-minded dialogue. Through seminars, policy programs, conferences and leadership development initiatives, the Institute and its international partners seek to promote nonpartisan inquiry and an appreciation for timeless values.

We help people become more enlightened in their work and enriched in their lives. Together we can learn one of the keys to being successful in business, leadership and life: balancing conflicting values in order to find common ground with our fellow citizens while remaining true to basic ideals.

Walter Isaacson

President & CEO

## THE ENTREPRENEURIAL SPIRIT – THE VISIONARY

Do you have what it takes to be a Social Entrepreneur: To create a Hybrid Organization:

To develop a Social Enterprise? Ask yourself – Am I a thermometer or a thermostat?

Let's examine the differences between the two.


Main Entry: **ther·mom·e·ter** ◀))

Pronunciation: \thə(r)-'mä-mə-tər\

Function: *noun*

Etymology:

> French *thermomètre,* from Greek *thermē* heat + French *-o-* + *-mètre* -meter

Date: 1633

: [15]an instrument for determining temperature; *especially* : one consisting of a glass bulb attached to a fine tube of glass with a numbered scale and containing a liquid (as mercury or colored alcohol) that is sealed in and rises and falls with changes of temperature


Main Entry: **clinical thermometer**

Function: *noun*

Date: 1875

: a thermometer for measuring body temperature that has a constriction in the tube above the bulb preventing movement of the column of liquid downward once it has reached its maximum temperature so that it continues to indicate the maximum temperature until the liquid is shaken back down into the bulb.


Main Entry: [1]**ther·mo·stat** ◀))

Pronunciation: \'thər-mə-ˌstat\

Function: *noun*

Date: 1831

---

[15] © 2007-2008 Merriam-Webster, Incorporated

: an automatic device for regulating temperature (as by controlling the supply of gas or electricity to a heating apparatus); *also* : a similar device for actuating fire alarms or for controlling automatic sprinklers

Main Entry: **thermostat**

Function: *transitive verb*

Date: 1924

: [16]to provide with or control the temperature of by a thermostat.

Highbeam Encyclopedia HighBeam™ Research, Inc. © Copyright 2008. All rights reserved.

thermometer   World Encyclopedia ... thermometer Instrument for measuring temperature . A mercury thermometer depends on the expansion of the metal mercury, which is held in a glass bulb connected to a narrow, graduated tube. Temperatures can also be measured by a gas thermometer and by a resistance thermometer that measures ... The word "thermometer" is a combination of "thermo," meaning "heat," and "meter," meaning "measure." So it truly is a "heat measurer".

Copyright 2003 The Topeka Capital-Journal

This material is published under license from the publisher through ProQuest Information and Learning Company, Ann Arbor, Michigan.

# thermostat

*From: World Encyclopedia  |  Date: 2005*

OXFORD
UNIVERSITY PRESS

- Print
- Digg
- del.icio.us

---

[16] © 2007-2008 Merriam-Webster, Incorporated. World Encyclopedia 2005, originally published by Oxford University Press 2005

thermostat [17]Device for maintaining a constant <u>temperature</u>. A common type contains a strip of two metals, one of which expands and contracts more than the other. At a set temperature, the strip bends and breaks the circuit. As it cools, the strip straightens, makes contact, and the heating begins again once the circuit is complete. Thermostats are used in air-conditioning systems and in refrigerators, ovens and water heaters.

© World Encyclopedia 2005, originally published by Oxford University Press 2005

Device that detects **temperature** changes for the purpose of maintaining the temperature of an enclosed area essentially constant.

The **thermostat** generates signals, usually electrical, to activate relays, <u>valves</u>, switches, and so on when the temperature rises above or falls below the desired value. **Thermostat**s are used to control the flow of fuel to a burner, of electric current to a heating or cooling unit, or of a heated or cooled gas or liquid into the area it serves. They are also used in fire-detection warning systems.
**thermostat.** (2008). In *Encyclopædia Britannica*. Retrieved January 7, 2008, from Encyclopædia Britannica Online: http://www.britannica.com/eb/article-9380604

[18]**Daniel Fahrenheit** born May 24, 1686, Gdask, Pol. died Sept. 16, 1736, The Hague, Dutch Republic. **German physicist and instrument maker.**

He spent most of his life in the Netherlands, where he devoted himself to the study of physics and the manufacture of precision meteorological instruments. He is best known for inventing a successful alcohol **thermometer** (1709) and mercury **thermometer** (1714) and for developing the <u>Fahrenheit</u> temperature scale, setting zero at the freezing point of an equal mixture of ice and salt. He discovered that water can remain liquid below its freezing point and that the boiling point of liquids varies with atmospheric pressure.

**Fahrenheit, Daniel.** (2008). In *Encyclopædia Britannica*. Retrieved January 7, 2008, from Encyclopædia Britannica Online: http://www.britannica.com/eb/article-9364152

According to the Thompson Chain-Reference Bible, "Where there is no vision, the people perish…" Proverbs 29:18a,[19] and when I hear and think of the word vision, I see an idea, concept or persuasion that literally impregnates one's soul. A vision is like a

---

[18] *Encyclopædia Britannica*. Retrieved January 7, 2008
[19] Thompson, 1988

prism; brilliant, majestically colorful and multifaceted. It goes far beyond the mind: it embraces and envelops the essence of your spirit. A vision literally wraps its arms around you, slides you between its folds, and seals you in its everlasting, manifold multiplicity of dimensions.

The visionary is a creative thinker that is farsighted, imaginative and inventive. The visionary is a risk taker because, more than likely, no one really understands the way the visionary thinks. Why he or she acts that way they do and where in the world do they come up with these "off the wall ideas". The visionary sees things that others just don't see. Visionaries are usually very positive people. They see the glass half full instead of half empty. They see possibilities instead of problems. They not only see potential, but they have the ability to maximize the potential in themselves, in others and in their organizations.

Basically everything that we take for granted in this world was invented, developed, created and implemented by a visionary. The street lights, stapler, light bulb, telephone, chair, desk, pen, pencil, eraser, car, round wheels, paper, wallets, clothing; computer, paper clip, telephone, cell phone: metrocard, ez-pass (go figure!), etc.; you name it someone thought of it and someone else thought they were crazy! Someone probably told them 'that will never sell'!!!! Now, we can't survive without most of these things.

Thermometers measure the temperature; they are affected by the surrounding environmental conditions and therefore, respond to heat or cold. It must be 'shaken' to return to it original state. It is a heat measurer. Thermometers are fragile as they are encased in glass. A thermostat is a regulator that determines the need for either heat or cold. Found in air conditioners, homes, burners, etc. they generate signals, usually electrical, and activate relays, <u>valves</u>, switches, and so on when the temperature rises above or falls below the desired value. **Thermostats** control the flow of fuel to a burner, of electric current to a heating or cooling unit, or of heated or cooled gas or liquid into the area it serves. They are also used in fire-detection warning systems.

So, do you want to be a determining factor? Do you want to be one to generate a new concept? Do you want to affect society in the social change arena? Or are you satisfied with being a part of the bunch (bananas) that respond as stimulated by economic and environmental needs? Responder or Controller? Thermostats use thermometers to determine the temperature. Thermometers are delegated and designed to discern and measure hot or cold and then record its findings in the tube so we can see the measurement. They are measurers by design! Thermometer or Thermostat? Choose well because lives are waiting in the balance and depending on you to take the leap of faith and discover your true destiny as a visionary and social entrepreneur.

## GENERAL RECOMMENDATIONS AND CONCLUSION

There is a real need for entrepreneurial minded visionaries that will address the social welfare needs globally. It's time to do some soul searching and address the call to leadership that may or may not have been laying dormant inside. Each day the world and billions of people contained therein, cry out in sheer desperation for help in their varied situations. Much has been done to alleviate the suffering and pain of many. Yet, there is room for so much more.

Below is part of an article by Peter Brinkerhoff. Read it. Digest it. Go to the website to read the entire article. http://www.allbusiness.com/specialty-businesses/non-profit-businesses/1017189-1.html . Then take the challenge if you can. The world is waiting.

# Why you need to be more entrepreneurial--and how to get started[20]

By Brinckerhoff, Peter
Publication: Nonprofit World
Date: Thursday, November 1 2001
HEADNOTE
ENTREPRENEURIAL spirit

HEADNOTE
Use these checklists to create an innovative, self-sufficient organization.

To serve people at the highest level, you must be a social entrepreneur, willing to take risks to serve people better. Social entrepreneurs have these characteristics:

* They are constantly looking for new ways to serve their constituencies and add value to existing services.

* They understand that all resource allocations are really stewardship investments.

* They weigh the social and financial return of each of these investments.

---

[20] © Copyright Society For Nonprofit Organizations Nov/Dec 2001. Provided by ProQuest Information and Learning. All rights Reserved.

\* They always keep mission first, but they know that they also need money; without it, there is no mission output.

\* They are willing to take reasonable risk on behalf of the people their organization serves.

Talk through these characteristics with your key staff and board. Focus particularly on two ideas: that expenditures are really investments and that risk is a good thing. It is vital to have widespread acceptance of these two concepts if your organization is to become and remain entrepreneurial.

# REFERENCES

Bornstein, David. (2004). How to Change the World: Social Entrepreneurs and the Power of New Ideas. Published by Oxford Press, Inc. New York, NY.

Brinckerhoff, Peter (2001).  Why you need to be more entrepreneurial--and how to get started. Publication: Nonprofit World, Vol. 19, No.6.  © Copyright Society For Nonprofit Organizations Nov/Dec 2001.  Provided by ProQuest Information and Learning. All rights Reserved.

Brooklyn Economic Development Corporation Copyright © 1997-2005

Dees, J. G. (1998), reformed and revised: May 30, 2001 [paper] PDF (5 pages) copy available at htttp://www.fuqua.duke.edu/centers/case/documents/deesSE.pdf.

Fahrenheit, Daniel. (2008). In *Encyclopædia Britannica.* Retrieved January 7, 2008, from Encyclopædia Britannica Online: http://www.britannica.com/eb/article-9364152

Johnson, Sherrill. (2003)  *"Young Social Entrepreneurs in Canada".*

Koppell, Jonathan. (2003). The Politics of Quasi-Government, Cambridge University Press

Rainey, Hal G. (1996). Understanding and Managing Public Organizations. Jossey-Bass

The Aspen Institute. Washington, D.C.  Copyright 2007 Aspen Institute. www.aspeninstitute.org

The Journal of Social Change. A refereed publication sponsored by Walden University. Volume 1, Issue 1 July 2006. Jim Goes, Ph.D., Walden University, Editor. Marilyn Simon, Ph.D., Walden University and Mark Gordon, Ph.D., Walden University, Associates Editors.  www.journalofsocialchange.org

UNICEF, *State of the World's Children 2000* (New York: United Nations Publications), 23-35

## ELECTRONIC RESOURCES

Wikipedia, the free encyclopedia.  www.wikipedia.org

www.hybridorganisations.com

www.virtueventures.com

# APPENDICES

**A.**

## Restoration Plaza

At the heart of Fulton Street is one of Bedford Stuyvesant's most familiar landmarks – the 300,000 square foot **Restoration Plaza**, owned and managed by Bedford Stuyvesant Restoration Corporation.

First built in the 1970s, Restoration Plaza retains some of the original shell of the historic row houses and a former milk bottling plant that stood on the property.

In addition to housing Restoration's administrative and program headquarters, Restoration Plaza is a major destination for education, commerce, and culture in Central Brooklyn. It is home to the Billie Holiday Theatre, Skylight Gallery and the Restoration Dance Theatre, and plays host to weddings, outdoor concerts and community events in it outdoor plaza.

Anchored by Super Foodtown and Applebee's, the Plaza offers a range of retail stores, professional services, non-profit organizations and educational institutions, all easily accessible to the community. Many of our tenants are locally-owned and operated.

Click here to browse or download our complete **Restoration Plaza Directory** (Link to Tenants Page).

### Renovations Now Underway!

While it has long been a commercial and cultural hub, Restoration Plaza's initial design has not kept pace with the expanding needs of the bustling Fulton Street corridor. In 2005, Restoration initiated a multi-phase redesign and renovation to enhance the Plaza's utility and appeal to businesses, their clients, shoppers, and patrons of the arts.

Learn more about the **Restoration Plaza Redesign** here. (Link to Redesign page and photos.)

### Leasing Space at Restoration Plaza

Thinking about relocating your business to the Plaza? Click here to learn more! (Link to Business Leasing Page)

We also rent space for a variety of community, corporate and private events. Click here to learn more. **(Link to Room Rentals)**

**B.**

# Brooklyn Economic Development Corporation

### Initiative for a Competitive Brooklyn

**Initiative for a Competitive Brooklyn**

**ABOUT THE INITIATIVE FOR A COMPETITIVE BROOKLYN** The Initiative for a Competitive Brooklyn (ICB) is a subsidiary of the Brooklyn Economic Development Corporation dedicated to increasing the sustainability and competitiveness of Brooklyn business. ICB was founded several years ago with support from many sponsors, including private corporations and foundations, local businesses and city and federal agencies. The original research which dictated ICB's first set of goals was by Harvard Professor Michael Porter and his group the Initiative for a Competitive Inner City (ICIC). Our mission, principles and method reflect that heritage.

- **MISSION:** The Initiative for a Competitive Brooklyn will enhance the competitiveness of Brooklyn firms in order to create a high and rising standard of living for Brooklyn residents.
- **PRINCIPLES:** ICB was founded on hard data and strives to achieve real, measurable results in specific clusters of the Brooklyn economy.
- **METHOD:** The ICB engages a team for each cluster. Teams represent a cross section of people, orgs and agencies involved in the cluster. ICB staff implements team recommendations.

**STRATEGIC BROOKLYN INDUSTRY CLUSTERS -** Four clusters of the Brooklyn economy were originally chosen for ICB: Health Care; Hospitality & Tourism; Real Estate, Construction & Development; and Food Processing. The first three have shown real growth, and, while it has declined, Food Processing remains an interesting and changing Brooklyn industry. Please look at our ICB Updated presentation for information on all the ICIC clusters and these 4 in particular.

**EMERGING BROOKLYN CLUSTERS -** Our Green Construction and Self-Employed Brooklyn reports outline some of the characteristics of clusters we see emerging in the borough today.

## C.

# The Meaning of "Social Entrepreneurship"

**J. Gregory Dees**
Original Draft: October 31, 1998
Reformatted and revised: May 30, 2001

The idea of "social entrepreneurship" has struck a responsive chord. It is a phrase well suited to our times. It combines the passion of a social mission with an image of business-like discipline, innovation, and determination commonly associated with, for instance, the high-tech pioneers of Silicon Valley. The time is certainly ripe for entrepreneurial approaches to social problems. Many governmental and philanthropic efforts have fallen far short of our expectations. Major social sector institutions are often viewed as inefficient, ineffective, and unresponsive. Social entrepreneurs are needed to develop new models for a new century.

The language of social entrepreneurship may be new, but the phenomenon is not. We have always had social entrepreneurs, even if we did not call them that. They originally built many of the institutions we now take for granted. However, the new name is important in that it implies a blurring of sector boundaries. In addition to innovative not-for-profit ventures, social entrepreneurship can include social purpose business ventures, such as for-profit community development banks, and hybrid organizations mixing not-for-profit and for-profit elements, such as homeless shelters that start businesses to train and employ their residents. The new language helps to broaden the playing field. Social entrepreneurs look for the most effective methods of serving their social missions.

Though the concept of "social entrepreneurship" is gaining popularity, it means different things to different people. This can be confusing. Many associate social entrepreneurship exclusively with not-for-profit organizations starting for-profit or earned-income ventures. Others use it to describe anyone who starts a not-for-profit organization. Still others use it to refer to business owners who integrate social responsibility into their operations. What does "social entrepreneurship" really mean? What does it take to be a social entrepreneur? To answer these questions, we should start by looking into the roots of the term "entrepreneur."

## Origins of the Word "Entrepreneur"

In common parlance, being an entrepreneur is associated with starting a business, but this is a very loose application of a term that has a rich history and a much more significant meaning. The term "entrepreneur" originated in French economics as early as the 17th and 18$^{th}$ centuries. In French, it means someone who "undertakes," not an "undertaker" in the sense of a funeral director, but someone who undertakes a significant project or activity. More specifically, it came to be used to identify the venturesome individuals who stimulated economic progress by finding new and better ways of doing things. The

French economist most commonly credited with giving the term this particular meaning is Jean Baptiste Say. Writing around the turn of the 19$_{th}$ century, Say put it this way, "The entrepreneur shifts economic resources out of an area of lower and into an area of higher productivity and greater yield." Entrepreneurs create value.

In the 20$_{th}$ century, the economist most closely associated with the term was Joseph Schumpeter. He described entrepreneurs as the innovators who drive the "creative-destructive" process of capitalism. In his words, "the function of entrepreneurs is to reform or revolutionize the pattern of production." They can do this in many ways: "by exploiting an invention or, more generally, an untried technological possibility for producing a new commodity or producing an old one in a new way, by opening up a new source of supply of materials or a new outlet for products, by reorganizing an industry and so on. "Schumpeter's entrepreneurs are the change agents in the economy. By serving new markets or creating new ways of doing things, they move the economy forward.

It is true that many of the entrepreneurs that Say and Schumpeter have in mind serve their function by starting new, profit-seeking business ventures, but starting a business is not the essence of entrepreneurship. Though other economists may have used the term with various nuances, the Say-Schumpeter tradition that identifies 2 entrepreneurs as the catalysts and innovators behind economic progress has served as the foundation for the contemporary use of this concept.

**Current Theories of Entrepreneurship**

Contemporary writers in management and business have presented a wide range of theories of entrepreneurship. Many of the leading thinkers remain true to the Say-Schumpeter tradition while offering variations on the theme. For instance, in his attempt to get at what is special about entrepreneurs, Peter Drucker starts with Say's definition, but amplifies it to focus on opportunity. Drucker does not require entrepreneurs to cause change, but sees them as exploiting the opportunities that change (in technology, consumer preferences, social norms, etc.) creates. He says, "this defines entrepreneur and entrepreneurship—*the entrepreneur always searches for change, responds to it, and exploits it as an opportunity.*" The notion of "opportunity" has come to be central to many current definitions of entrepreneurship. It is the way today's management theorists capture Say's notion of shifting resources to areas of higher yield. An opportunity, presumably, means an opportunity to create value in this way. Entrepreneurs have a mind-set that sees the possibilities rather than the problems created by change.

For Drucker, starting a business is neither necessary nor sufficient for entrepreneurship. He explicitly comments, "Not every new small business is entrepreneurial or represents entrepreneurship." He cites the example of a "husband and wife who open another delicatessen store or another Mexican restaurant in the American suburb" as a case in point. There is nothing especially innovative or change-oriented in this. The same would be true of new not-for-profit organizations. Not every new organization would be entrepreneurial. Drucker also makes it clear that entrepreneurship does not require a profit motive. Early in his book on *Innovation and Entrepreneurship*, Drucker asserts, "No better text for a *History of Entrepreneurship* could be found than the creation of the modern university, and especially the modern American university." He then explains what a major innovation this was at the time. Later in the book, he devotes a chapter to entrepreneurship in public service institutions. Howard Stevenson, a leading theorist of entrepreneurship at Harvard Business School, added an element of resourcefulness to the opportunity-oriented definition based on research he conducted to determine what distinguishes entrepreneurial management from more common forms of "administrative" management. After identifying several dimensions of difference, he suggests defining the heart of entrepreneurial management as "the pursuit of opportunity without regard to resources currently controlled." He found that entrepreneurs not only see and pursue opportunities that elude administrative managers; entrepreneurs do not allow their own initial resource endowments to limit their options. To borrow a metaphor from Elizabeth Barrett Browning, their reach exceeds their grasp. Entrepreneurs mobilize the resources of others to achieve their entrepreneurial objectives. Administrators allow their existing resources and their job descriptions to constrain their visions and actions. Once again, we have a definition of entrepreneurship that is not limited to business start-ups.

**Differences between Business and Social Entrepreneurs**

The ideas of Say, Schumpeter, Drucker, and Stevenson are attractive because they can be as easily applied in the social sector as the business sector. They describe a mind-set and a kind of behavior that can be manifest anywhere. In a world in which sector boundaries are blurring, this is an advantage. We should build our understanding of social entrepreneurship on this strong tradition of entrepreneurship theory and research. Social entrepreneurs are one species in the genus entrepreneur. They are entrepreneurs with a social mission. However, because of this mission, they face some distinctive challenges and any definition ought to reflect this.

For social entrepreneurs, the social mission is explicit and central. This obviously affects how social entrepreneurs perceive and assess opportunities. Mission-related impact becomes the central criterion, not wealth creation. Wealth is just a means to an end for social entrepreneurs. With business entrepreneurs, wealth creation is a way of measuring value creation. This is because business entrepreneurs are subject to market discipline, which determines in large part whether they are creating value. If they do not shift resources to more economically productive uses, they tend to be driven out of business.

Markets are not perfect, but over the long haul, they work reasonably well as a test of private value creation, specifically the creation of value for customers who are willing and able to pay. An entrepreneur's ability to attract resources (capital, labor, equipment, etc.) in a competitive marketplace is a reasonably good indication that the venture represents a more productive use of these resources than the alternatives it is competing against. The logic is simple. Entrepreneurs who can pay the most for resources are typically the ones who can put the resources to higher valued uses, as determined in the marketplace. Value is created in business when customers are willing to pay more than it costs to produce the good or service being sold. The profit (revenue minus costs) that a venture generates is a reasonably good indicator of the value it has created. If an entrepreneur cannot convince a sufficient number of customers to pay an adequate price to generate a profit, this is a strong indication that insufficient value is being created to justify this use of resources. A re-deployment of the resources happens naturally because firms that fail to create value cannot purchase sufficient resources or raise capital. They go out of business. Firms that create the most economic value have the cash to attract the resources needed to grow.

Markets do not work as well for social entrepreneurs. In particular, markets do not do a good job of valuing social improvements, public goods and harms, and benefits for people who cannot afford to pay. These elements are often essential to social entrepreneurship. That is what makes it social entrepreneurship. As a result, it is much harder to determine whether a social entrepreneur is creating sufficient social value to justify the resources used in creating that value. The survival or growth of a social enterprise is not proof of its efficiency or effectiveness in improving social conditions. It is only a weak indicator, at best.

Social entrepreneurs operate in markets, but these markets often do not provide the right discipline. Many social-purpose organizations charge fees for some of their services. They also compete for donations, volunteers, and other kinds of support. But the discipline of these "markets" is frequently not closely aligned with the social entrepreneur's mission. It depends on who is paying the fees or providing the resources, what their motivations are, and how well they can assess the social value created by the venture. It is inherently difficult to measure social value creation. How much social value is created by reducing pollution in a given stream, by saving the spotted owl, or by providing companionship to the elderly? The calculations are not only hard but also contentious. Even when improvements can be measured, it is often difficult to attribute them to a specific intervention. Are the lower crime rates in an area due to the Block Watch, new policing techniques, or just a better economy? Even when improvements can be measured and attributed to a given intervention, social entrepreneurs often cannot capture the value they have created in an economic form to pay for the resources they use. Whom do they charge for cleaning the stream or running the Block Watch? How do they get everyone who benefits to pay? To offset this value-capture problem, social entrepreneurs rely on subsidies, donations, and volunteers, but this further muddies the waters of market discipline. The ability to attract these philanthropic resources may provide some indication of value creation in the eyes of the resource providers, but it is not a very reliable indicator. The psychic income people get from giving or volunteering is likely to be only loosely connected with actual social impact, if it is connected at all.

**Defining Social Entrepreneurship**

Any definition of social entrepreneurship should reflect the need for a substitute for the market discipline that works for business entrepreneurs. We cannot assume that market discipline will automatically weed out social ventures that are not effectively and efficiently utilizing resources. The following definition combines an emphasis on discipline and accountability with the notions of value creation taken from Say, innovation and change agents from Schumpeter, pursuit of opportunity from Drucker, and resourcefulness from Stevenson. In brief, this definition can be stated as follows:

*Social entrepreneurs play the role of change agents in the social sector, by: • Adopting a mission to create and sustain social value (not just private value),*

*• Recognizing and relentlessly pursuing new opportunities to serve that mission,*

- *Engaging in a process of continuous innovation, adaptation, and learning,*

- *Acting boldly without being limited by resources currently in hand, and*

- *Exhibiting heightened accountability to the constituencies served and for the outcomes created.*

This is clearly an "idealized" definition. Social sector leaders will exemplify these characteristics in different ways and to different degrees. The closer a person gets to satisfying all these conditions, the more that person fits the model of a social entrepreneur. Those who are more innovative in their work and who create more significant social improvements will naturally be seen as more entrepreneurial. Those who are truly Schumpeterian will reform or revolutionize their industries. Each element in this brief definition deserves some further elaboration. Let's consider each one in turn.

*Change agents in the social sector:* Social entrepreneurs are reformers and revolutionaries, as described by Schumpeter, but with a social mission. They make fundamental changes in the way things are done in the social sector. Their visions are bold. They attack the underlying causes of problems, rather than simply treating symptoms. They often reduce needs rather than just meeting them. They seek to create systemic changes and sustainable improvements. Though they may act locally, their actions have the potential to stimulate global improvements in their chosen arenas, whether that is education, health care, economic development, the environment, the arts, or any other social field.

*Adopting a mission to create and sustain social value:* This is the core of what distinguishes social entrepreneurs from business entrepreneurs even from socially responsible businesses. For a social entrepreneur, the social mission is fundamental. This is a mission of social improvement that cannot be reduced to creating private benefits (financial returns or consumption benefits) for individuals. Making a profit, creating wealth, or serving the desires of customers may be part of the model, but these are means to a social end, not the end in itself. Profit is not the gauge of value creation; nor is customer satisfaction; social impact is the gauge. Social entrepreneurs look for a long-term social return on investment. Social entrepreneurs want more than a quick hit; they want to create lasting improvements. They think about sustaining the impact.

*Recognizing and relentlessly pursuing new opportunities:* Where others see problems, social entrepreneurs see opportunity. They are not simply driven by the perception of a social need or by their compassion, rather they have a vision of how to achieve improvement and they are determined to make their vision work. They are persistent. The models they develop and the approaches they take can, and often do, change, as the entrepreneurs learn about what works and what does not work. The key element is persistence combined with a willingness to make adjustments as one goes. Rather than giving up when an obstacle is encountered, entrepreneurs ask, "How can we surmount this obstacle? How can we make this work?"

*Engaging in a process of continuous innovation, adaptation, and learning:* Entrepreneurs are innovative. They break new ground, develop new models, and pioneer new approaches. However, as Schumpeter notes, innovation can take many forms. It does not require inventing something wholly new; it can simply involve applying an existing idea in a new way or to a new situation. Entrepreneurs need not be inventors. They simply need to be creative in applying what others have invented. Their innovations may appear in how they structure their core programs or in how they assemble the resources and fund their work. On the funding side, social entrepreneurs look for innovative ways to assure that their ventures will have access to resources as long as they are creating social value. This willingness to innovate is part of the modus operandi of entrepreneurs. It is not just a one-time burst of creativity. It is a continuous process of exploring, learning, and improving. Of course, with innovation comes uncertainty and risk of failure. Entrepreneurs tend to have a high tolerance for ambiguity and learn how to manage risks for themselves and others. They treat failure of a project as a learning experience, not a personal tragedy.

*Acting boldly without being limited by resources currently in hand:* Social entrepreneurs do not let their own limited resources keep them from pursuing their visions. They are skilled at doing more with less and at attracting resources from others. They use scarce resources efficiently, and they leverage their limited resources by drawing in partners and collaborating with others. They explore all resource options, from pure philanthropy to the commercial methods of the business sector. They are not bound by sector norms or traditions. They develop resource strategies that are likely to support and reinforce their social missions. They take calculated risks and manage the downside, so as to reduce the harm that will result from failure. They understand the risk tolerances of their stakeholders and use this to spread the risk to those who are better prepared to accept it.

*Exhibiting a heightened sense of accountability to the constituencies served and for the outcomes created*: Because market discipline does not automatically weed out inefficient or ineffective social ventures, social entrepreneurs take steps to assure they are creating value. This means that they seek a sound understanding of the constituencies they are serving. They make sure they have correctly assessed the needs and values of the people they intend to serve and the communities in which they operate. In some cases, this requires close connections with those communities. They understand the expectations and values of their "investors," including anyone who invests money, time, and/or expertise to help them. They seek to provide real social improvements to their beneficiaries and their communities, as well as attractive (social and/or financial) return to their investors. Creating a fit between investor values and community needs is an important part of the challenge. When feasible, social entrepreneurs create market-like feedback mechanisms to reinforce this accountability. They assess their progress in terms of social, financial, and managerial outcomes, not simply in terms of their size, outputs, or processes. They use this information to make course corrections as needed.

## Social Entrepreneurs: A Rare Breed

Social entrepreneurship describes a set of behaviors that are exceptional. These behaviors should be encouraged and rewarded in those who have the capabilities and temperament for this kind of work. We could use many more of them. Should everyone aspire to be a social entrepreneur? No. Not every social sector leader is well suited to being entrepreneurial. The same is true in business. Not every business leader is an entrepreneur in the sense that Say, Schumpeter, Drucker, and Stevenson had in mind. While we might wish for more entrepreneurial behavior in both sectors, society has a need for different leadership types and styles. Social entrepreneurs are one special breed of leader, and they should be recognized as such. This definition preserves their distinctive status and assures that social entrepreneurship is not treated lightly. We need social entrepreneurs to help us find new avenues toward social improvement as we enter the next century.

*J. Gregory Dees is the Miriam and Peter Haas Centennial Professor in Public Service at Stanford's Graduate School of Business and an Entrepreneur In Residence at the Kauffman Center for Entrepreneurial Leadership. The Kauffman Center for Entrepreneurial Leadership provided the funding for this paper. The paper has benefited tremendously from comments and suggestions by the members of the Social Entrepreneurship Funders Working Group, particularly Suzanne Aisenberg, Morgan Binswanger, Jed Emerson, Jim Pitofsky, Tom*

*Reis, and Steve Roling.*

Nonprofit World, Vol. 19, No. 6
12

To serve people at the highest level, you must be a social entrepreneur, willing to take risks to serve people better. Social entrepreneurs have these characteristics::

• They are constantly looking for new ways to serve their constituencies and add value to existing services.

• They understand that all resource allocations are really stewardship investments.

• They weigh the social and financial return of each of these investments.

• They always keep mission first, but they know that they also need money; without it, there is no mission output.

• They are willing to take reasonable risk on behalf of the people their organization serves.

Talk through these characteristics with your key staff and board. Focus particularly on two ideas: that expenditures are really investments and that risk is a good thing. It is vital to have widespread acceptance of these two concepts if your organization is to become and remain entrepreneurial.

# ENTREPRENEURIAL *spirit*
## Figure 1. Social Entrepreneurship Self-Assessment Yes No

Has the organization investigated (or is it currently pursuing) nontraditional business activities to supplement income?

Does the organization weigh the mission return and the financial return of every investment (and view expenditures as investments)?

Have the staff and board identified the organization's core competencies?
Is the organization constantly looking for ways to match these competencies with the markets' wants?

Does the organization have a list of criteria for new service ideas?

Does the organization have a social entrepreneurship team?

Are program options or change opportunities free of restriction from facilities or debt you already have?

Are the concerns of staff and service recipients acknowledged and addressed when change is initiated?

Are core values and the mission statement discussed when changes are considered?

Have you discussed with board and staff the organizational willingness to take risk?

Is change initiated as an improvement without criticizing what has been done before?

Is innovation encouraged and are rewards provided at evaluation time?

**Total of column score**

Add each column up and put the answer here ➡

**TOTAL SCORE**

Add total scores from Yes and No columns and put the answer here ➡

SCORING ANALYSIS: 32-26 Excellent, 25-20 Very Good, 19-12 Adequate
Less than 12—You need to focus more on creating an entrepreneurial organization.

# Why You Need to Be More Entrepreneurial—And How to Get Started

*Use these checklists to create an innovative, self-sufficient organization.*
BY PETER BRINCKERHOFF
November • December 2001
13

## Figure 2. Social Entrepreneurship Readiness Checklist

| Area | Readiness Item | Yes | No | Don't Know |
|------|----------------|-----|-----|-----------|

**Mission** Have the staff and board reviewed the idea of business development in relation to the organization's mission statement?

Are revisions or updates of the mission necessary?

Have you decided on the mission uses for the business and the mission uses for any profits?

**Risk** Have the board and staff discussed the risk inherent in new business development?

Have limits been set on venture capital to put at risk?

Do your board and staff view resource allocations as investments rather than expenditures?

Do your board and staff understand that the desired outcome for a not-for-profit business is a mix of mission return and financial return?

**Systems** Does the organization have personnel and finance policies that have been revised in the past 24 months?

Does the organization have a strategic plan that is current?

Does the organization have the information systems, payroll, accounts payable and receivable systems that can accommodate growth?

Is the organization's financial accounting software able to track multiple projects and/or businesses?

**Skills** Are all of the following skills available within the staff and governing volunteers: planning, budgeting, pricing, marketing, project management?

Are skills and experience available within the industry or area that you have chosen to pursue?

Has the management team made the commitment to allow talented and experienced individuals to use their skills to develop the new business?

Have you generated a list of your organization's core competencies?

**Space** Is there readily available appropriate physical space to house the business?

Is there adequate equipment, wiring, plumbing, ventilation, security, and lighting for the business?

**Finance** Has the organization as a whole been profitable the past three years?

Does the organization have at least 90 days of cash or cash equivalents on hand?

Does the organization have an excellent relationship with its banker?

Does the organization have a line of credit?

Does the organization have a current ratio of 1.0 or higher?

Does the organization have a debt to net worth of .3 or less?

Are you sure your funders won't penalize you for any net income from the business?

## TOTALS

Add up the number of Yes, No and Don't Know answers and put the total in the column to the right ➡

If more than eight answers are "no" or "don't know," go back over the questions, and take the time to improve your score. Your organization must be in good shape before you develop a new, and inevitably risky, venture.

Nonprofit World, Vol. 19, No. 6
14

The next step is to develop a business venture to support your mission and create a financially empowered organization. First ask yourself the questions in Figures 1 and 2 to be sure your organization is ready. Then follow these steps:

**1. Review your mission statement.**
Do all staff and board members know what your mission statement is?

Do they agree it's the best possible description of what you do and the world you want to live in?

The questions in Figure 3 will help you decide if you need to change your mission statement. If no, follow the suggestions in Figure 4.

**2. Assess your willingness to take risk.**
Meet with your board to explore the concept of acceptable risk. Note that risk is the engine of innovation, and innovation is crucial to keeping up with the wants and expectations of your markets. Good stewardship requires you to take reasonable risks in light of your financial condition, your markets, and your organizational culture.

**3. Generate business ideas.**
Gather staff for a brainstorming session. Ask for ideas for a business related to your organization's primary purpose. When you've created a list, develop criteria against which to weigh each idea. For example, you might give priority to businesses that you can start up in less than six months, that require an investment of less than $10,000, and that have a direct social

impact. The combination of criteria will be up to you, but by establishing what is important now, you can weigh all ideas without upsetting people whose ideas aren't followed up.

### 4. Develop preliminary feasibility studies.
Write three to five pages, reviewing each potential business, its market, and what kind of services are being provided in this market. Ask, "Can we do this? Do we have (or can we get) the resources to do it?"

### 5. Develop a final feasibility study.
After narrowing your business ideas down to the most feasible one, describe in detail the service you want to provide, how you will provide it, the barriers to success, and how you will overcome those barriers.

### 6. Define your market.
Next, focus on the market for your new business. Who are those people? Where are they? How any of them are there? Why do they want your service? Be as specific as you can.

### 7. Define your target market.
Target a particular segment of your market for your highest research and customer-service efforts.

### 8. List the five core wants of the target market.
The issue isn't what people *need* but what they *want*. How do you know what they want? Did you ask them, or are you making (perhaps dangerous) assumptions?

### 9. List your core competencies.
Do you have the core competencies (things you are really, really good at) to match up with your market's wants? If not, you may need to go back a step and change your target market, or find ways to strengthen or acquire certain competencies.

### 10. Decide how you will reach your target market.
If you're entering a new market, how will you establish a beachhead? What tactics will you use to establish relations with your market? Examples could include trade show presentations, cold calls, referrals, advertising, or some other outreach function.

### 11. Decide on the mission outcomes of your business.
This is a crucial step. Now that you have defined your business, what do you expect the mission outcomes to be? Some specific mission service? Profit to do more direct mission?

### 12. Review key financials.
How much start-up money are you putting at risk? Where will this money come from? What will the initial size of your business be in terms of revenue, units of production, employees, and space? What will your fixed and variable costs be?

### 13. Develop a business plan.
Include a description of your organization, your new business, and the market for your new service. Detail your marketing plan, including an evaluation of potential pitfalls. Provide a financial plan, including cash flow estimates, projected income and expenses, a balance sheet, and break-even analysis.

### 14. Implement your business plan.

A new business is always a risk, but going through this planning process reduces that risk. Following these steps assures that you will be taking prudent risks on behalf of the people you serve. That's what entrepreneurship is all about.

## Figure 3. Mission Statement Self-Assessment Yes No

Has your mission statement been reviewed by your board and staff within the past two years?

Ask five staff at random what the mission statement is. Do all five get reasonably close?

Ask four board members what the mission statement is. Do all four get reasonably close?
Does staff use the mission statement as an aid to decision-making and management? Are copies on the table at every meeting?

Is there a vision statement associated with your mission statement?
Is the mission statement short—less than 50 words?

Does the board refer to the mission statement when considering adding or dropping services? Are copies on the table at every board meeting?

Do you celebrate the success of your mission at every staff meeting?

Do staff and board consider, and verbalize, that expenditures are really investments in mission?

Is your mission statement posted in the organization? Included in marketing materials? Stated in personnel policies?

Is the current mission statement on file with the IRS?

Is the mission statement used as a criterion in some manner in your personnel evaluations?
**Total of column score**

Add each column up and put the answer here ➡

**TOTAL SCORE—MISSION STATEMENT**

Add total scores from Yes and No columns and put the answer here ➡
SCORING ANALYSIS: 34-27 Excellent, 26-20 Very Good, 19-10 Adequate
Less than 10—Meet with staff and board to create a mission everyone embraces.
November • December 2001
15

**Selected References**
Brinckerhoff, Peter, "But Is It Really
Feasible?", *Nonprofit World,* Vol. 16, No. 6.
Brinckerhoff, Peter, "How to Write
Your Business Plan," *Nonprofit World,*
Vol. 17, No. 2.
Brinckerhoff, Peter, *Mission-Based
Management, Videotape.*
Brinckerhoff, Peter, "Starting a Business:
Too Risky for Your Organization?", *Nonprofit
World,* Vol. 16, No. 4.
Muehrcke, Jill, ed., CD-ROM of *Nonprofit
World* Articles.
Muehrcke, Jill, ed., *Enterprise, Leadership
Series.*
Steckel, Richard, "Developing an
Entrepreneurial Vision," *Nonprofit World,*

Vol. 11, No. 3.
Wilson, Leslie, "Is It Feasible? The Prime
Question in Venture Planning," *Nonprofit
World,* Vol. 6, No. 5.
These resources are available from the
Society's Resource Center, 608-274-9777, Ext.
221, www.danenet.org/snpo.
*Peter Brinckerhoff is president of Corporate
Alternatives, inc. (CAi), a firm specializing
in nonprofit organizations (2707 West
Washington, Suite C, Springfield, IL
62702). He is the author of* Mission-Based
Management *and* Mission-Based Management:
An Organizational Development
Workbook (John Wiley & Sons), *from which
this article is adapted.*

## Figure 4. **Mission Statement Checklist**
**Here are some things you can do to improve your mission statement:**
Review your mission statement at the management level.
Ask these questions:

_____ Does the mission use correct, current language?

_____ Does the mission describe adequately who we serve? (demographics)

_____ Does the mission describe adequately where we work? (geographics)

_____ Does the mission show focus?

_____ Does the mission excite us?

_____ Can we get our mission down to less than 50 words?

_____ Do we need a vision associated with our mission?

_____ Do we need to write down a statement of values along with our mission?

Ask the staff to discuss not just the mission statement wording, but what it means to them.
Meet with the board and staff, discuss your findings, and talk about necessary changes.
Any adopted changes should be sent to the IRS with details of the board meeting, and a listing of
the board members who voted for and against the changes.

The mission statement should be evident everywhere: on the wall, on marketing materials, on the
back of staff business cards, on screen savers, on the annual report, on the table at board and
staff meetings.

Nonprofit World • Volume 19, Number 6 November/December 2001
Published by the Society for Nonprofit Organizations
6314 Odana Road, Suite 1, Madison, WI 53719 • (608) 274-9777
www.danenet.org/snpo

ARTICLE

# Understanding Multi-purpose Hybrid Voluntary Organizations: The Contributions of Theories on Civil Society, Social Movements and Non-profit Organizations by YEHESKEL HASENFELD_ & BENJAMIN GIDRON

_Department of Social Welfare, UCLA School of Public Affairs, USA, __Israeli Center for Third Sector Research, Ben-Gurion University of the Negev, Israel

ABSTRACT

The paper offers a theoretical framework to study the conditions that lead to the emergence of multi-purpose hybrid voluntary organizations and the factors that influence their ability to mobilize resources and enlist commitment. These organizations are characterized by four interrelated attributes: (a) they set out as their mission to uphold and promote cultural values that are typically at variant with dominant and institutionalized values; (b) they offer services to members and the public that express their distinct values, using the services as a model and catalyst for social change; (c) in addition to their instrumental goals, they aim to meet the expressive and social identity needs of their members by promoting a collective identity; and (d) they evolve into hybrid organizations by having multiple purposes—combining to various degrees goals of value change, service provision and mutual-aid. Because they deliberately combine features of volunteer-run associations, social movements and non-profit service organizations, we articulate a theoretical framework that melds concepts and propositions from the various theoretical perspectives used to study each of these organizational forms. We argue that the expanded theoretical framework offers a more comprehensive and dynamic view of civil society and a better perspective to the study of third sector organizations.

KEY WORDS: Hybrid voluntary organizations, social movements, civil society, non-profit organizations

Journal of Civil Society

Vol. 1, No. 2, 97–112, September 2005

Correspondence Address: Yeheskel Hasenfeld, Department of Social Welfare, UCLA School of Public Affairs, 3250 PPB, Los Angeles, CA 90095, USA. Email: zekeh@ucla.edu

ISSN 1744-8689 Print=1744-8697 Online=05=020097–16 # 2005 Taylor & Francis
DOI: 10.1080=17448680500337350

Introduction

Traditionally, research on third sector organizations1 has been segmented into three distinct theoretical perspectives that can be roughly labeled 'civil society', 'social movement' and 'non-profit sector'. Civil society scholars, such as Putnam (2000) and Smith (1997), focus primarily on autonomous volunteer-run associations characterized by citizen participation and horizontal network relations (e.g., social clubs, mutual aid associations).

Students of social movements (e.g., McAdam et al., 1996) have concentrated on organizations that use protest and extra institutional means to achieve social change. Researchers on the non-profit sector, such as Galaskiewicz and Bielefeld (1998), Salamon (1995) and Gronjberg (1993), study formally structured and legally recognized non-profit service organizations that are tax-exempt and are prohibited from distributing profits. Therefore, each research tradition focuses on an organizational form that is dominant and characteristic of the class of organizations it studies, and this form drives much of the research enterprise.

Yet, it is becoming increasingly clear that many third sector organizations, as they evolve over time, incorporate multiple purposes and structural features from all three prevailing forms. Examples of such organizations include racial, ethnic and gender-based organizations (Minkoff, 1995), religious charitable organizations (Allahyari, 2000), women's non-profit organizations (Bordt, 1998), peace and conflict resolution organizations (Gidron et al., 2002) and social influence organizations (Knoke & Wood, 1981).

These organizations are distinguished by four interrelated attributes. Firstly, they set out as their mission to uphold and promote cultural values that are typically at variant with dominant and institutionalized values (Goodwin et al., 2001). Secondly, they offer services to members and the public that express their distinct values, using the services as a model and catalyst for social change. Thirdly, in addition to their instrumental goals, they aim to meet the expressive and social identity needs of their members by promoting a collective identity (Gamson, 1991; Schmitt & Martin, 1999). Fourth, and most importantly, they evolve into hybrid organizations by having multiple purposes, combining to various degrees goals of value change, service provision and mutual-aid (Minkoff, 1995, 2002), and a deliberate mix of organizational forms borrowed from volunteer-run associations, social movements and non-profit service organizations. We denote these organizations as 'multi-purpose hybrid organizations'. Our definition should not be confused with similar terms used (e.g., multiple-product) to describe non-profit organizations that pursue for-profit enterprises (see Weisbrod, 1998), or organizations with multiple service domains and clients (see D'Aunno et al., 1991). What distinguishes these multi-purpose hybrid organizations from strictly social movement organizations, non-profit service organizations or volunteer-run associations is that they combine key features from all three: (a) they seek to bring about social change, though not necessarily through protest and other non-institutional means; (b) the services they provide, such as social and educational, are a strategy for social change; (c) their internal structure is a mix of collectivist and bureaucratic elements (Bordt, 1998). The importance of these organizations as purveyors of cultural values, as catalysts of social change and as providers of invaluable services to their members and the general public cannot be underestimated.

Studies of multi-purpose hybrid organizations (see Hyde 1992; Bordt, 1998; Minkoff 2002), including our own comparative study of peace and conflict resolution organizations 98 Y. Hasenfeld & B. Gidron (Gidron et al., 2002), grapple with three major research questions. Firstly, they try to understand the societal conditions that give rise to these organizations. Secondly, they want to understand how such organizations, despite their unconventional values, are able to mobilize resources to sustain themselves. Thirdly, they want to explain the ability of such organizations to enlist and maintain the commitment of their members.

Such studies have tended to rely mostly on organizational theories such as population ecology, resource dependency and institutional theory. These theories are typically applied to analyze non-profit service organizations. Yet, in doing so, they are neither able to fully capture the complexity of the context that give rise to these organizations nor can they adequately address the distinctive issues they face in mobilizing resources and enlisting commitment. We have encountered the same theoretical difficulties in our own study of peace and conflict resolution organizations (P/CROs) in Northern Ireland, Israel/Palestine and South Africa. Briefly, the comparative study consists of a sample of ten P/CROs in each region. Extensive case data were collected on the founding, mission, leadership and membership, resources and structure of each organization.2 We initially conceptualized P/CROs as non-profit service organizations and applied a political-economy/institutional theory to explain their emergence, their capacity to mobilize resources and ability to sustain commitment of members. However, we quickly came to realize the inadequacy of such a theory to account for the unique features of these organizations and the complex environments in which they exist.

Therefore, our aim in this paper is threefold. First and foremost, we want to offer a more comprehensive theoretical perspective to explain emergence, resource mobilization and commitment. Secondly, we want to show that a synthesis of concepts and propositions from the three theoretical perspectives—civil society, social movement and non-profit service sector—can provide a better theoretical framework to address these issues. In doing so, we also rely on research findings and analytic insights gained from our comparative study.

Thirdly, we want to suggest that the general field of third sector organizations, with its complex array of organizational forms, may benefit from a greater theoretical integration of the three perspectives. An Expanded Conception of Civil Society

A first step in formulating a more comprehensive theoretical framework to study multipurpose hybrid organizations is to recognize that they deliberately incorporate a mix of organizational features from volunteer-run associations, social movements and nonprofit service organizations. Therefore, to better locate them among the organizational forms that constitute civil society, we start with the distinction that Foley and Edwards (1996) make between what they term 'Civil Society I' and 'Civil Society II'. The first, exemplified by Berger et al. (1996) and Putnam (2000), refers to volunteer-run associations, networks of civic engagement and the production of social capital in fostering collective trust and in strengthening democracy. It purposefully excludes associations and networks that generate conflict or challenge the state. The second refers to groups that do challenge the state. These include not only movements that struggle against authoritarian regimes (Cohen & Arato, 1992; Bernhard, 1993), but also the new social movements that are concerned with social, cultural and quality-of-life issues, such as peace, human and citizenship rights, globalization and the environment (Kriesi et al., 1995).

Understanding Multi-purpose Hybrid Voluntary Organizations 99

Notably missing from their classification is the non-profit service sector which is also a vital aspect of civil society. Moreover, increasingly researchers point to social movement, advocacy and challenging organizations as significant constituents of the non-profit sector (Jenkins, 1987; McCarthy et al., 1991). Hybrid organizations that combine both non-profit service and protest or advocacy functions play a prominent role in meeting the needs and advancing the cause of marginalized groups (Hyde, 1992; Bordt, 1998; Minkoff, 2002).

Indeed, it is quite common for these social movements to become incorporated as nonprofit organizations (Cress, 1997). We should add that social protest and advocacy organizations can have many elements characteristic of Civil Society I. These include reliance on dense social networks and grassroots infrastructures, the accumulation of social capital by powerless groups, the creation of a collective identity and the expansion of the public sphere by promoting debates and dialogues (Minkoff, 1997).

To recognize that volunteer-run associations, social movements and non-profit service organizations actually represent different dimensions of civil society is to build on the insightful distinctions made by Foley and Edwards (1996) and add the non-profit service sector as a third dimension of civil society. Such an expansion enables us to locate multi-purpose hybrid organizations at the intersection of these three dimensions. As we show below, the expanded conception of civil society also directs us to theoretical constructs and findings from all three dimensions to better explain the emergence of multipurpose hybrid organizations, their capacity to mobilize resources and ability to enlist commitment. Moreover, it also enables us address more adequately the dynamic changes that organizations may undergo as they traverse through the complex field of civil society.

One way to capture the variety of organizations that constitute civil society is to classify them along two axes that determine their purpose and organizational form (see also Kriesi, 1996, p. 153). The first axis is the relationship between the organization and the state. It influences not only the emergence of different organizations but, particularly, their capacity and strategies to mobilize resources. The second refers to the organization's relationship to its constituents. It influences organizational efforts to enlist and maintain Table 1. Types of organization by relationship to state and constituencies Neutral (Civil Relationship to the state Oppositional (Civil Society II) Co-operative/ dependent (Civil Society I) Regime Policy Society III) Relationship to constituents Full Participation Self-help group Counterculture, Anarchists Community advocacy group Neighborhood crime watch, PTO Limited participation Sports club South Africa Black Sash Women rights movement; Amnesty International Salvation Army; Trade association Token participation Museum South Africa Institute of Race Relations ACLU Hospital; Research center 100 Y. Hasenfeld & B. Gidron commitment (McCarthy & Walker, 2004). We propose that the purpose or institutional role of the organization is largely defined by its relationship to the state, which may be neutral, oppositional or cooperative. Relationship to constituents, which range on a continuum from total participation to token participation, defines the internal organizational structure (see also Kriesi, 1996; Galaskiewicz &Bielefeld, 1998). Table 1 presents the results of our classification.

Civil Society I consists of organizations that have a neutral relationship to the state. While they may view themselves as contributing to the 'good society', they generally focus on the well-being of their own members. If they interact with the state it is in order to obtain an appropriate legal status (e.g., tax exempt status). They assume a neutral or indifferent stance toward state political institutions and policies since these seldom concern their activities. They neither openly support nor oppose them. Social clubs and self-help groups are prime examples of such organizations.

Civil Society II consists of organizations that arise in direct opposition to state political institutions and policies with an explicit mandate to change them by using non-conventional political means (thus excluding strictly lobby organizations). These include various local and national social movement organizations such as civil rights, anti-abortion or anti-globalization movements. We distinguish between two types of social movement organizations—transforming and reforming (Lofland, 1996).

Transforming social movements oppose state regimes and seek to replace them with alternative regimes. Examples may include pro-democracy or anti-global economy movements. In our study, almost all peace organizations in South Africa were transforming social movements that sought to overturn the Apartheid regime. In contrast, reforming social movements do not oppose state regimes per se but seek to alter their policies, as is the case with pro-choice, pro-life organizations or civil rights movements. All the peace organizations in Israel were reforming social movements, as they were careful not to challenge the legitimacy of the regime. Opposing state regimes or policies does not necessarily indicate that the challengers do not interact with state officials or representatives of political elites. However, the challengers typically operate outside the normally instituted political processes.3

Finally, Civil Society III consists of organizations that legitimate and reinforce state regimes and policies through their programs and activities. Indeed, they often depend on the state both for legitimacy and fiscal resources (Salamon, 1995). These organizations include mostly non-profit service organizations that receive a tax-exempt status and obtain from the state a significant portion of their resources. Examples are hospitals and social service agencies. They also include various lobby organizations and interest groups, such as trade and professional associations, that attempt to influence public policy to favors their constituencies (Laumann & Knoke, 1987). It is worth noting that organizations dependent on the state may also oppose certain state policies. For example, religious-based organizations may obtain public funding to assist poor families, but may still oppose state policies regarding abortion.

It is important to emphasize that the boundaries among the three dimensions of civil society are fluid. Throughout their life course, organizations may alter their relations to the state with concomitant changes in their institutional role. For example, self-help groups may expand and receive state support in order to offer services to a broader group of beneficiaries. Others may turn into counter-culture movements. Social movement organizations may succeed in changing state policies and become non-profit service Understanding Multi-purpose Hybrid Voluntary Organizations 101 organizations and vice versa (Minkoff, 2002). Similarly, non-profit service organizations, such as churches, under particular political opportunities, may mobilize their resources for social movement activities (Kurzman, 1998). Indeed, there seems to be a typical life cycle trajectory of multi-purpose hybrid organizations. They often begin as volunteer-run associations, are transformed into social movement organizations and, if they are successful in mobilizing resources, become non-profit service organizations (see Hyde, 1992; Schmitt & Martin, 1999).

The state too may change its political institutions and polices, resulting in altered relations with various organizations. In South Africa, for example, organizations that were in opposition to the Apartheid regime found themselves in a co-operative and often dependent relationship with the post-Apartheid Government (Habib & Taylor, 1999). It is precisely the fluidity in the movement of organizations across the complex landscape of civil society and the periodic changes in the polity that generates many hybrid forms. Turning to the relationships of organizations with their constituents, total participation characterizes organizations in which constituents both control and run them, as in the case of self-help groups and the celebrated bowling leagues. The archetype is volunteer-run associations, which Smith (1997) terms as "grassroots associations". Limited participation characterizes organizations in which constituents define and shape policies and approve programs but rely on paid staff to carry out daily operations, as in the case of labor unions or the National Organization for Women. Such organizations are characterized by a powerful elected board that represents their constituents. This was the modal pattern for P/CROs in all three regions. Token participation characterizes organizations that are controlled and run by paid staff, as in the case of most non-profit service organizations.

While they may have constituents on their board of directors or as volunteers, they provide only token participation. Surprisingly, in our study about 40% of the P/CROs were controlled by paid staff, mostly in Northern Ireland and South Africa. Relations with constituencies are also fluid and may change over time. Some theorists have argued that over time surviving organizations tend to move toward the professional model (see DiMaggio & Anheier, 1990). Others have shown that a strong commitment to collectivist beliefs can sustain full participation by members (see Rothschild-Whitt, 1979; Bloomfield, 1994). In our own study, a few of the peace organizations were indeed able to retain their collectivist structure.

Finally, as we detail below, this expanded conception of civil society presupposes a social system in which (a) the power of the state is checked; (b) the public sphere is institutionalized; and (c) it comprises of networks of associations and organizations expressing diverse interests. Explaining Emergence, Resource Mobilization and Commitment To address these issues, we have reviewed the three theoretical perspectives with an eye to selecting what we consider to be their signal contributions in addressing these research questions. For example, like social movements, multi-purpose hybrid organizations espouse values that challenge established institutional rules. Therefore, research findings on the importance of the political context in facilitating or impeding the formation of social movements would be relevant to this set of organizations. Similarly, because these organizations also provide concrete services, research on non-profit service 102 Y. Hasenfeld & B. Gidron organizations could shed light on how such organizations mobilize needed resources.

Finally, since multi-purpose hybrid organizations also address the expressive needs of their members, we look toward findings on how volunteer-run associations use social networks to recruit members and sustain their commitment to the organization. Also, in this process we are guided by the theoretical and empirical challenges presented by our own comparative study. We have looked for the efficacy of each perspective in helping us explain how, in each region, the P/CROs emerged, mobilized resources and maintained commitment.

Emergence

There is a consensus among civil society researchers that third sector organizations can form when two interrelated societal conditions exist. The first refers to the existence of a public sphere. Somers (1993, p. 589) defines it as "a contested participatory site in which actors with overlapping identities as legal subjects, citizens, economic actors, and family and community members, form a political body and engage in negotiations and contestations over political and social life". The second refers to the proliferation or richness of associational life (see Putnam et al., 1993).

That was clearly the case in our own study. In all three regions, the formation of the peace and conflict resolution organizations was correlated with the expansion of the public sphere and the non-profit service sector: The reforms instituted in the mid 1980s by P. W. Botha in South Africa that permitted multiracial parties and legalized the African trade unions; the new Law of Amutot (associations) enacted in Israel in 1980, facilitating the establishment of such entities; and the increasing encouragement by the UK Government, backed with financial subsidies, of the work of local inter-community organizations in Northern Ireland.

In other words, we argue that multi-purpose hybrid organizations cannot emerge in societies that lack these two pre-requisites—a public sphere and a proliferation of third sector organizations. Indeed, the very existence of a non-profit service sector with its diverse array of organizations that are relatively independent of the state is a clear manifestation of a viable public sphere. In contrast, third sector organizations formed or controlled by the state do not contribute to a viable public sphere. For example, different accounts on the non-profit sector in the former Soviet Bloc (see Fric et al., 1998; Saulean & Epure, 1998) suggest that existing organizations were few and heavily controlled by the state. In another account of volunteer-run associations during the Nazi regime (Bauer, 1990) a similar picture emerges. This is not surprising as totalitarian regimes tend to limit "personal choices and forms of human involvement" (Starr, 1990, p. 37). Starr adds that "a vital civil society requires more than a rich variety of voluntary associations and independent centers of power; it also needs a rich sphere of public discussion that engages society's diverse classes and groups".4

Proposition 1. The larger the public sphere and the greater the richness of associational life, the greater the emergence of multi-purpose hybrid organizations Still, for multi-purpose hybrid organizations to arise also requires a particular political milieu, or what researchers of social movements call a 'political opportunity structure' (Tarrow, 1994; McAdam, 1996; Rucht, 1996). Because these organizations engage in advocacy and social movement activities, their capacity to do so presupposes a political Understanding Multi-purpose Hybrid Voluntary Organizations 103 milieu with certain characteristics. Accordingly, research on social movements (see Tarrow, 1994; Della Porta & Rucht, 1995) shows that they are more likely to emerge when: (a) the political system is open and competitive; (b) political elites are divided; (c) use of threats and coercive means by the regime is checked; and (d) the organizations have access to elite allies. Jenkins et al. (2003) find that African-American protest increased when Government was divided, when the political strength of Northern Democrats increased, and when Republican Presidents were pressured to take a procivil rights stance because of the Cold War. Interestingly, increase in Black representatives in Congress lowered protest.

Our own study reaffirms the importance of political opportunities and threat. While most of the P/CROs, in all three regions, emerged as the conflict intensified, their emergence signaled elite political realignments. In Israel, it was a change in the ruling Government coalition that gave greater voice to peace advocates. In Northern Ireland, under its direct rule, the UK Government increased its involvement by funding bridging community associations. In South Africa, the Apartheid regime initiated in the 1980s several liberalization reforms, such as allowing colored and Indian political representation, encouraging the creation of a Black middle class, and easing the restrictions on voluntary associations. In all three regions, these political changes also led to curbs on state use of coercive power, although in South Africa, the increase in protest brought a backlash in the form of a declaration of a state emergency (Gidron et al., 2002, pp. 42–46).

Proposition 2. Multi-purpose hybrid organizations are more likely to emerge when the political system is more competitive, political elites are divided, the state repressive power is checked, and the organizations have access to elite allies Resource Mobilization For organizations to survive they have to mobilize members, financial resources and legitimacy. Theories on volunteer-run associations and social movement organizations stress the importance of social networks in the mobilization of members. Undoubtedly, one of the lasting contributions of civil society theories is in highlighting the importance of social networks and the resulting social capital both as the sustenance of volunteer-run associations and as a mobilizing force for new associations. It is the glue that keeps associations together, and it is a powerful resource social movements use to mobilize members for collective action. Putnam (2000) distinguishes between bonding and bridging social networks, the first promotes single identity and ethnic associations, and the second encourages the formation of broad-based associations. Relevant to our study, there is significant evidence to suggest that associations formed by bridging social networks are more effective in reducing conflict and promoting peace (Varshney, 2002).

Research on social movement mobilization also points to social networks, including networks density, frequency of contact and shared ideologies as key to mobilizing members (see McAdam, 1988; McCarthy et al., 1991). In our own study we find evidence that members were recruited through extensive reliance on friendship and professional networks and the use of social capital. This resulted in a high degree of social homogeneity of the membership. Israeli peace organizations were comprised primarily of Jews from the middle and upper classes and those of Ashkenazi/European origin. South African organizations consisted primarily of White middle class 104 Y. Hasenfeld & B. Gidron English-speaking staff and members. Only in Northern Ireland did the peace organizations display a significant degree of cross-ethnic membership drawn from working and middle class backgrounds.

Proposition 3. The greater the access of multi-purpose hybrid organizations to social networks the greater their ability to mobilize members and garner support

Civil society scholars also emphasize the importance of 'civic skills' as a mobilizing resource. As articulated by Brady et al., (1995, p. 273) "Citizens who can speak and write well or who are comfortable organizing and taking part in meetings are likely to be more effective when they get involved in politics". These skills can be honed through participation in the workplace and various third sector organizations. Hence, the availability of potential members with high civic skills provides the leadership stock needed for effective organization building. Indeed, in our study, in all three regions, leaders were recruited with strong 'civic skills'. In Northern Ireland, leaders were experienced union activists or local community organizers. In Israel, many were former military officers and active members of political parties. In South Africa, a number of the leaders were intellectuals connected to the academic and research institutions as well as members of established third sector organizations.

Proposition 4. The greater the ability of multi-purpose hybrid organizations to recruit leaders with extensive civic skills the greater their chances to survive

Analogous to social networks, the embeddedness of the organization in an interorganizational network is a major determinant of its capacity to mobilize economic and political resources. Minkoff (2002) has shown that the ability of identity-based advocacy organizations to survive depends on adopting organizational forms that are institutionalized in their organizational ecology. Others have suggested that the ability of social movement organizations to secure legitimacy and stable fiscal seems to depend on the development of formal internal structures (Zald & McCarthy, 1987; Kriesi, 1996).

In our own study, almost all the P/CROs in the three regions developed a formal structure. While many began as loosely and informally organized associations, at the time of our study almost all had paid staff and acquired a legal status of a non-profit organization (Meyer, 1999). Undoubtedly, the peace organizations that survived beyond their founding stage were those whose structure became more formalized and professionalized. Still, in keeping with their collectivist ideology (Rothschild-Whitt, 1979), three of the organizations, all in Israel, adopted a collectivist structure and five (three in Northern Ireland) adopted both formal and collectivist features. These findings are replicated in studies of non-profit service organizations whose survival and capacity to obtain resources depends on (a) interorganizational linkages with major sources of legitimacy and funding (Baum & Oliver, 1991); and (b) embeddedness of dominant institutional norms in their structure (DiMaggio & Anheier, 1990).

One interesting finding from our own study was the dependence of the P/CROs on funding sources that were not indigenous to the societies in which they operated. In both South Africa and Israel, where the stance of these organizations had been primarily oppositional to the state or its policies, the major sources of funding were foreign— whether governments, private foundations or religious organizations. In Northern Ireland, where many of the groups studied had worked to establish inter-community relations in order to contain the violence of paramilitary groups, they were fiscally supported by the UK Government, which Understanding Multi-purpose Hybrid Voluntary Organizations 105 promoted such projects. Dependence on such funding sources also increased the need to formalize and professionalize the organization. Clearly, the advantage of reliance on external funding networks for the P/CROs was to buffer them from local retributions. Researchers who study hybrid organizations emphasize the process of institutionalization as a key determinant of their survival (Hyde, 1992; Minkoff, 2002). By institutionalization they mean the processes by which the organization conforms to dominant cultural values by giving them expression in their organizational structure (Scott, 1995).

Institutionalization poses a dilemma to multi-purpose hybrid organizations because their values are at variant with dominant cultural belief systems. Hence, they attempt to legitimize their values by linking them and appealing to commonly accepted cultural symbols such as personal liberty and citizenship rights. For example, in the US, pro-abortion organizations rationalize their values by appeal to personal liberty and freedom from state interference. In Germany, in contrast, they appeal to the state responsibility to protect the well-being of women (Ferree, 2003). In other words, these organizations frame their particular values in ways that resonate with dominant cultural beliefs (Snow & Benford, 1988). As we show below, this was particularly evident in our study where most of the P/CROs adopted values that resonated with institutionalized cultural beliefs. Proposition 5(a). The greater the connectedness of multi-purpose hybrid organizations to other organizations that control important resources (e.g., members, funds, legitimacy, and technical expertise) the greater their chances of survival Proposition 5(b). The survival of multi-purpose hybrid organizations depends on their ability to develop a formal structure Proposition 5(c). The survival of multi-purpose hybrid organizations depends on their embracing mainstream cultural symbols Commitment

Since the issue of commitment is central to both volunteer-run associations and social movement organizations, there has been considerable cross-fertilization between the two research traditions. Borrowing from social psychological studies on organizational commitment (see Meyer & Allen, 1997), researchers have examined the incentives that motivate individuals to join and participate in these organizations (Klandermans, 1997). At the social psychological level, commitment is a consequence of the accumulation of social capital and the trust that it promotes (Anheier & Kendall, 2002). It is also reinforced by personal fulfillment that comes from participation. As Gamson (1992, p. 56) notes "Participation in social movements frequently involves enlargement of personal identity for participation and offers fulfillment and realization of the self". This is particularly the case in multi-purpose hybrid organizations because they explicitly aim to respond to the expressive needs of their members and to foster a collective identity. In her study of women's health centers, Hyde (1992) notes the conscientious efforts of these organizations to forge a collective feminist identity that responded to the expressive needs of the members.

Researchers on social movement organizations also emphasize the importance of a shared set of symbols or "frames". According to Snow and Benford (1988, p. 198), frames "assign meaning to and interpret relevant events and conditions in ways that are intended to mobilize 106 Y. Hasenfeld & B. Gidron potential adherents and constituents, to garner bystander support, and to demobilize antagonists". Frames typically consist of a definition of the problem, prognosis and a call for action. Snow and Benford (1988) propose that the more these frames resonate with the belief systems held by potential and actual members, the more these frames will be incorporated into their own social networks and 'lifeworld', and the greater will be their commitment to the social movement.\

Similarly, studies of non-profit service organizations point to the importance of organizational ideologies and culture in maintaining the commitment of staff members to the organization (Weick, 1995; Glisson & James, 2002). In particular, the ideologies promote a collective rationale for the existence and importance of the organization, and provide a shared set of beliefs that justify its activities. Karabanow (1999), for example, recounts how a youth shelter had developed a 'pro-kid' culture that directed and controlled the emotional work between workers and clients. Because most of the workers perceived their work as an extension of their own personal and intrinsic being, their values resonated with the organizational culture thus reinforcing each other.

In our own study, the frames selected by the P/CROs varied by region, echoing the nature of the conflict, the political context in which it was embedded, and the available cultural tool kits. In South Africa, most of organizations framed the problem as the very nature of the Apartheid regime. The solution was seen in the establishment of a new political regime based on democratic, just and non-racial principles. The call for action was to de-legitimize the regime. Commitment of members was based on that shared vision of a non-racial, just and democratic society. It was a vision that was consonant with the personal values of many of the members who were highly educated and from an English-speaking background. In Israel, for most of the peace organizations the diagnosis was the occupation of the West Bank and Gaza and its danger to the Israeli social and moral order. The prognosis was to end the occupation and the call for action was to recognize the right of the Palestinians to self-determination. Individual commitment was sustained because the principle of self-determination and human rights, coupled with an affirmation of loyalty to the state and the Zionist ideology, resonated well with the liberal cultural values and identities of the members. In Northern Ireland, a majority of the organizations defined the problem as attitudinal and interpersonal prejudice. The prognosis was interpersonal tolerance of religious and ethnic differences. The call for action was to promote dialogue and mutual understanding between members of the two communities.

Many Catholics and Protestants could support the peace organizations because these frames confirmed their own daily experiences of living together, and because they abhorred the violence perpetrated by the paramilitaries.

Proposition 6(a). The greater the ability of the multi-purpose hybrid organizations to respond to the expressive and social identity needs of their members and forge a collective identity, the greater the commitment and trust of members in the organization

Proposition 6(b). The greater the resonance of the frames adopted by the multi-purpose hybrid organizations with the personal beliefs of their members and supporters, the greater their commitment to the organization

In Table 2 we summarize the contributions of each theoretical perspective in identifying and explaining the factors that influence the emergence of multi-purpose hybrid organizations, their capacity to mobilize resources and their ability to generate commitment.

Understanding Multi-purpose Hybrid Voluntary Organizations 107
We wish to stress that integrating the theoretical and empirical insights from all three perspectives not only enriches research on multi-purpose hybrid organizations, but more broadly the study of third sector organizations. As noted earlier, many non-profit service organizations evolve over time from either a volunteer-run association or a social movement. These early organizational forms and the values they embody leave an indelible mark on subsequent organizational developments and transformations.

Therefore, a fuller explanation of the mission, inter-organizational relations, services and structures of non-profit service organizations often requires the incorporation and integration of theoretical and empirical constructs from these other research traditions. In our own study, we first began with an analytic framework typically used to study nonprofit service organizations. Yet, as we had collected more data about the P/CROs, we came to recognize that they share many features with social movement organizations. We also noted that several started as volunteer-run associations. We realized that we were unable to adequately explain the conditions leading to the emergence of the P/CROs, their strategies to mobilize resources and members, their internal structure and their choices of actions lest we turn to the other theories. For example, we used concepts such as public sphere and political opportunity structure to explain the emergence of the P/CROs. Similarly, we employed concepts such as social networks, interorganizational relations and institutionalization to explain how they mobilized resources and attained legitimacy. Finally, we relied heavily on notions of personal fulfillment, cultural frames and organizational ideologies to understand the commitment of members and the choices of action strategies.

It is also clear from our analysis that whether one studies volunteer-run associations, social movement organizations or non-profit service organizations, the researcher quickly encounters a broadly diverse and heterogeneous set of organizations. Therefore, no single theoretical perspective can hope to fully explain the evolution, survival, structure and membership patterns. Indeed, adherence to a single perspective may cause the researcher to ignore important findings that could enrich the analysis. Kenneth Andrews and Bob Edwards (2004) make a similar argument regarding the study of advocacy organizations. They also call for the need to integrate theories on socials movement, interest groups and non-profits. As they point out "the compartmentalization of research within sub-fields and disciplines means that core ideas and findings go unnoticed by scholars studying similar phenomena" (Andrews & Edward, 2004, p. 500).

We could not agree more. Table 2. Conceptual contributions of civil society, social movement and non-profit service sector research Civil society Social movement Non-profit sector Emergence Public sphere; Civic culture Political opportunity structure (POS) Infrastructure of non-profits Resource mobilization Social network; Social capital; Civic skills Social network; Interorganizational linkages; Formalization of structure Interorganizational linkages; Institutionalization Commitment Personal fulfillment Shared frame Organizational ideologies 108 Y. Hasenfeld & B. Gidron

Conclusion

We have shown that the study of the emergence of multi-purpose hybrid organizations and their strategies to mobilize resources and enlist commitment can benefit from the integration of concepts, theoretical insights and findings from each of the three research traditions on civil society, social movements and the non-profit service sector. Indeed, we argue that the three perspectives complement each other, and that studies of volunteer-run associations, social movements and non-profit service organizations can be greatly enriched from such integration. However, to do so requires, first and foremost, that we adopt a broader conception of civil society, as we have proposed in this paper. In particular, the dynamic relationship between the dimensions of civil society and the transformation paths that third sector organizations may undergo as they move from one dimension to another requires that we also broaden our theoretical boundaries.

As this paper suggests, it is time for the intellectual walls that separate civil society, social movement and non-profit service sector theories to come down. Several studies, including our own, have shown that the terrains covered by each of the three research traditions often overlap and have many similar features. Indeed, one of our main arguments is that third sector organizations are dynamic entities. Throughout their life cycle, they move back and forth through the different configurations of civil society, especially as they respond to macro-social, political and cultural forces that affect the balance and relations among its constituent elements. Each theoretical perspective may be particularly useful in explaining a specific phase in the evolution of these organizations. We propose that melding the unique contributions of each research tradition in explaining the three major organizational issues addressed in this paper—emergence, resource mobilization and commitment—is an important step toward their theoretical cross-fertilization.

Notes
1. The literature on this category of organizations uses various terms such as 'non-profit organizations', 'voluntary associations' and 'civil society organizations' among others. The idea in all cases is that these organizations are neither a constituent of the public sector nor a part of the profit-making sector.

2. For complete details on the methodology and findings see Gidron et al. (2004).

3. That was the case for most of the peace organizations in Israel, which used back channels to interact with political elites.

4. We are also cognizant of the fact that rich associational life may be exploited by totalitarian political parties to gain hegemony (see Kwon, 2004).

References
Allahyari, R. A. (2000) Visions of Charity: Volunteer Workers and Moral Community (Berkeley: University of California Press).

Almond, G. A. & Verba, S. (1989) The Civic Culture: Political Attitudes and Democracy in Five Nations (Newbury Park: Sage Publications).

Andrews, K. T. & Edwards, B. (2004) Advocacy organizations in the US political process, Annual Review of Sociology, 30, pp. 479–508.

Anheier, H. & Kendall, J. (2002) Interpersonal trust and voluntary associations: examining three approaches, The British Journal of Sociology, 53, pp. 343–362.

Bauer, R. (1990) Voluntarism, nongovernmental organizations and public policy in the Third Reich, Non-profit and Voluntary Sector Quarterly, 19, pp. 199–214.

Understanding Multi-purpose Hybrid Voluntary Organizations 109

Baum, J. A. & Oliver, C. (1991) Institutional linkages and organizational mortality, Administrative Science Quarterly, 36, pp. 187–218.

Berger, P. L., Neuhaus, R. J. & Novak, M. (1996) To Empower People: From State to Civil Society (2nd ed.) (Washington, DC: American Enterprise Institute).

Bernhard, M. (1993) Civil society and democratic transition in East Central Europe, Political Science Quarterly, 108, pp. 307–326.

Bloomfield, K. (1994) Beyond sobriety: the cultural significance of Alcoholic Anonymous, Non-profit and Voluntary Sector Quarterly, 23, pp. 21–40.

Bordt, R. L. (1998) The Structure of Women's Non-profit Organizations (Bloomington, ID: Indiana University Press).

Brady, H. E., Verba, S. & Schlozman, K. L. (1995) Beyond Ses: a resource model of political participation, The American Political Science Review, 89, pp. 271–294.

Cohen, J. L. & Arato, A. (1992) Civil Society and Political Theory (Cambridge, MA: The MIT Press).

Cress, D. M. (1997) Non-profit incorporation among movements of the poor: pathways and consequences for homeless social movement organizations, The Sociological Quarterly, 38, pp. 343–360.

Della Porta, D. & Rucht, D. (1995) Left–libertarian movements in context: a comparison of Italy and West Germany, 1965–1990, in: J. C. Jenkins & B. Klandermans (Eds) The Politics of Social Protest, pp. 229–272 (Minneapolis, MN: University of Minnesota Press).

DiMaggio, P. J. & Anheier, H. K. (1990) The sociology of non-profit organizations and sectors, Annual Review of Sociology, 16, pp. 137–159.

D'Aunno, T., Sutton, R. I. & Price, R. H. (1991) Isomorphism and external support in conflicting institutional environments: a study of drug abuse treatment units, Academy of Management Journal, 34, pp. 636–661.

Ferree, M. M. (2003) Resonance and radicalism: feminist framing in the abortion debate in the United states and Germany, American Journal of Sociology, 109, pp. 304–344.

Foley, M. W. & Edwards, B. (1996) The paradox of civil society, Journal of Democracy, 7, pp. 38–53. Fric, P., Deverova, L. & Parjas, P. (1998) Defining the Non-profit Sector: The Czech Republic (Baltimore: John Hopkins Comparative Non-profit Sector Project).

Galaskiewicz, J. & Bielefeld, W. (1998) Non-profit Organizations in an Age of Uncertainty (New York, NY: Aldine De Gruyter).

Gamson, W. (1991) Commitment and agency in social movements, Sociological Forum, 6, pp. 27–50.

Gamson, W. (1992) The social psychology of collective action, in: A. Morris & C. M. Mueller (Eds) Frontiers in Social Movement Theory, pp. 53–76 (New Haven, CT: Yale University Press).

Gidron, B., Katz, S. N. & Hasenfeld, Y. (2002) Mobilizing for Peace: Conflict Resolution in Northern Ireland, Israel/Palestine, and South Africa (New York: Oxford University Press).

Glisson, C. & James, L. R. (2002) The cross-level effects of culture and climate in human service teams, Journal of Organizational Behavior, 23, pp. 767–794.

Goodwin, J., Jasper, J. M. & Polletta, F. (Eds) (2001) Passionate Politics: Emotions and Social Movements (Chicago: University of Chicago Press).

Gronbjerg, K. A. (1993) Understanding Non-profit Funding: Managing Revenues in Social Services And
Community Development Organizations (San Francisco: Jossey-Bass).
Habib, A. & Taylor, R. (1999) South Africa: Anti-Apartheid NGOs in transition, Voluntas, 10, pp. 73–82.

Hyde, C. (1992) The ideational system of social movement agencies: an examination of feminist health centers, in: Y. Hasenfeld (Ed.) Human Services as Formal Organizations, pp. 121–144 (Newbury Park, CA: Sage Publications).

Jenkins, J. C. (1987) Non-profit organizations and policy advocacy, in: W. W. Powell (Ed.) The Non-profit Sector: A Research Handbook, pp. 296–318 (New Haven, CT: Yale University Press).

Jenkins, J. C., Jacobs, D. & Agnone, J. (2003) Political opportunities and African-American protests, 1948–1997, American Journal of Sociology, 109, pp. 277–303.

Karabanow, J. (1999) When caring is not enough: emotional labor and youth shelter workers, Social Service Review, 73, pp. 340–357.

Klandermans, B. (1997) The Social Psychology of Protest (Oxford: Blackwell).

Knoke, D. & Wood, J. R. (1981) Organized for Action (New Brunswick, NJ: Rutgers University Press).

Kriesi, H. (1996) The organizational structure of new social movements in a political context, in: D.McAdam, J. D. McCarthy & M. N. Zald (Eds) Comparative Perspectives on Social Movements, pp. 152–184 (New York: Cambridge University Press).
110 Y. Hasenfeld & B. Gidron

Kriesi, H., Koopmans, R., Dyvendak, J. W. & Giugni, M. G. (1995) New Social Movements in Western Europe: A Comparative Analysis (Minneapolis: University of Minnesota Press).

Kurzman, C. (1998) Organizational opportunity and social movement mobilization: a comparative analysis of four religious movements, Mobilization, 3, pp. 23–49.

Kwon, H. K. (2004) Associations, civic norms, and democracy: revisiting the Italian case, Theory and Society, 33, pp. 135–166.

Laumann, E. O., & Knoke, D. (1987) The Organizational State: Social Choice in National Policy Domains (Madison: University of Wisconsin Press).

Lofland, J. (1996) Social Movement Organizations (New York: Aldine de Gruyter).

McAdam, D. (1988) Micromobilization contexts and recruitment to activism, International Social Movement Research, 1, pp. 125–154.

McAdam, D. (1996) Political opportunities: conceptual origins, current problems, future directions, in: D. McAdam, J. D. McCarthy & M. N. Zald (Eds) Comparative Perspectives on Social Movements, pp. 23–40 (New York: Cambridge University Press).

McAdam, D., McCarthy, J. D. & Zald, M. N. (Eds) (1996) Comparative Perspectives on Social Movements (New York: Cambridge University Press).

McCarthy, J., Britt, D. & Wolfson, M. (1991) The institutional channeling of social movements in the United States, Research in Social Movements, Conflicts and Change, 13, pp. 45–76.

McCarthy, J. D. & Walker, E. T. (2004) Alternative organizational repertoires of poor people social movement organizations, Non-profit and Voluntary Sector Quarterly, 33, pp. 97–119.

Meyer, J. P. & Allen, N. J. (1997) Commitment in the Workplace: Theory, Research, and Application (Thousand Oaks: Sage Publications).

Meyer, M. B. (1999) The role of ideology in directing organizational behavior: Peace and conflict resolution organization in Israel/Palestine, Northern Ireland, and South Africa, PhD Dissertation, Department of Social Welfare, The University of California, Los Angeles.

Minkoff, D. C. (1995) Organizing for Equality: The Evolution of Women's and Racial-ethnic Organizations in America, 1955–1985 (New Brunswick, NJ: Rutgers University Press).

Minkoff, D. C. (1997) Producing social capital, American Behavioral Scientist, 40, pp. 606–619.

Minkoff, D. C. (2002) The emergence of hybrid organizational forms: combining identity–based service provision and political action, Non-profit And Voluntary Sector Quarterly, 31, pp. 377–401.

Putnam, R. D. (2000) Bowling Alone: The Collapse and Revival of American Community (New York: Simon & Schuster).

Putnam, R. D., Leonardi, R. & Nanetti, R. (1993) Making Democracy Work: Civic Traditions in Modern Italy (Princeton, N.J.: Princeton University Press).

Rothschild-Whitt, J. (1979) The collectivist organization: an alternative to rational bureaucratic models, American Sociological Review, 44, pp. 509– 527.

Rucht, D. (1996) The impact of national contexts on social movement structures: a cross-movement and cross-national comparison, in: D. McAdam, J. D. McCarthy & M. N. Zald (Eds) Comparative Perspectives on Social Movements, pp. 185–204 (New York, NY: Cambridge University Press).

Salamon, L. M. (1995) Partners in Public Service: Government–Non-profit Relations in the Modern Welfare State (Baltimore, MD: Johns Hopkins University Press).
Saulen, D. & Epure, C. (1998) Defining the Non-profit Sector: Romania (Baltimore: John Hopkins Comparative Non-profit Sector Project).

Schmitt, F. E. & Martin, P. Y. (1999) Unobtrusive mobilization by an institutionalized rape crises center, Gender & Society, 13, pp. 364–384.

Scott, W. R. (1995) Institutions and Organizations (Thousand Oaks, CA: Sage Publications).

Smith, D. H. (1997) Grassroots associations are important: some theory and a review of impact literature, Nonprofit and Voluntary Sector Quarterly, 26, pp. 269–306.

Snow, D. & Benford, R. (1988) Ideology, frame resonance, and participant mobilization, International Social Movement Research,, 1, pp. 197–217.

Somers, M. R. (1993) Citizenship and the place of the public sphere: law, community and the political culture in the transition to democracy, American Sociological Review, 58, pp. 587–620.

Starr, P. (1990) The new life of the liberal state: privatization and the restructuring of state–society relations, in: J. Waterbury & E. Suleiman (Eds) Public Enterprise and Privatization (Boulder, CO: Westview Press).

Tarrow, S. (1994) Power in Movement: Social Movements, Collective Action and Mass Politics in the Modern State (New York: Cambridge University Press). Understanding Multi-purpose Hybrid Voluntary Organizations 111

Varshney, A. (2002) Ethnic Conflict and Civic Life: Hindus and Muslims in India (New Haven, CT: Yale University Press).

Weick, K. E. (1995) Sensemaking in Organizations (Thousand Oaks: Sage Publications).

Weisbrod, B. A. (1988) The Non-profit Economy (Cambridge, MA: Harvard University Press).

Weisbrod, B. A. (Ed.) (1998) To Profit or Not to Profit: The Commercial Transformation of the Non-profit Sector (New York: Cambridge University Press).

Zald, M. N. & McCarthy, J. D. (1987) Social movement industries: competition and conflict among SMOs, in: M. N. Zald & J. D. McCarthy (Eds) Social Movements in an Organizational Society, pp. 161–180 New Brunswick, NJ: Transaction Books).
112 Y. Hasenfeld & B. Gidron

Lightning Source UK Ltd.
Milton Keynes UK
01 October 2009

144376UK00001B/83/P